BIGFOOT
AND ADAPTATION

BY TERRY COLLINS • ILLUSTRATED BY CRISTIAN MALLEA

Consultant:
Patrik Nosil, PhD
Assistant Professor
Department of Ecology and
Evolutionary Biology
University of Colorado

CAPSTONE PRESS
a capstone imprint

GRAPHIC LIBRARY

Graphic Library is published by Capstone Press,
1710 Roe Crest Drive, North Mankato, Minnesota 56003.
www.capstonepub.com

Library of Congress Cataloging-in-Publication Data
Collins, Terry.
Bigfoot and adaptation / by Terry Collins.
    p. cm.—(Graphic library. Monster science)
Includes bibliographical references and index.
Summary: "In cartoon format, uses bigfoot to explain the science of adaptation"—Provided
by publisher.
ISBN 978-1-4296-6579-7 (library binding)
ISBN 978-1-4296-7327-3 (paperback)
1. Adaptation (Biology)—Juvenile literature. 2. Sasquatch—Juvenile literature. I. Title.
QH546.C59 2012
001.944—dc22   2011004484

Editor
Anthony Wacholtz

Art Director
Nathan Gassman

Designer
Ashlee Suker

Production Specialist
Eric Manske

TABLE OF
CONTENTS

CHAPTER 1

WHAT ARE ADAPTATIONS?

The planet Earth is 4.54 billion years old. The human population numbers in the billions.

Now add all living things, and the number of life forms grows into the trillions.

Earth is the thriving home to millions of different plant and animal species.

All of these species are connected through evolution. Evolution is the change of living things over a period of time.

SCRATCH SCRATCH

Evolution accounts for the wide variety of species. All living things have evolved. Their bodies and behaviors have changed over many generations.

HUMAN EVOLUTION

WHERE I FIT IN?

These changes are known as adaptations. Adaptations are changes in a living thing's physical structure or behavior over many generations.

BIGFOOT ADAPTED GOOD!

Adaptations have happened throughout history. But the idea of adaptation was only first proposed about 150 years ago.

In 1859 Charles Darwin introduced the theory of evolution. Darwin proposed that all species evolved from a common ancestor.

As a young man, Darwin traveled with the crew of the HMS *Beagle* from 1831 to 1836. On his trip, he collected many kinds of plants and animals.

Darwin realized the animals he discovered on his trip had different traits from animals in the same species.

He realized not all members within a species are exactly the same. They had adapted to their environments.

Darwin saw that the adaptations could be in color, strength, speed, or size. With each new generation, the stronger qualities were passed down from parents to children.

SON HAS BIGFOOT'S HAIRY CHEST!

The organisms with the "best" traits thrived and produced more offspring. This idea became known as natural selection, or "survival of the fittest."

BIGFOOT NO IN HERE!

Darwin later wrote about what he saw in his book *The Origin of Species*.

CHAPTER 2

PHYSICAL ADAPTATIONS

What we know about adaptations has come a long way since Darwin.

There are two main types of adaptations: physical and behavioral.

Physical adaptations are changes to the body of a living thing. These changes allow the living thing to reproduce, eat, and defend itself.

They also allow living creatures to thrive in their environments. Adaptations such as fins and gills let fish swim and breathe underwater.

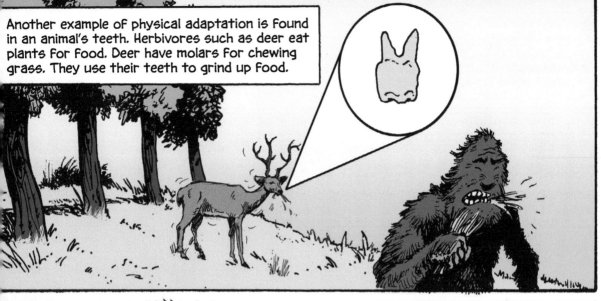

Another example of physical adaptation is found in an animal's teeth. Herbivores such as deer eat plants for food. Deer have molars for chewing grass. They use their teeth to grind up food.

Carnivores such as lions are meat eaters. They have sharp teeth that help them attack their prey and tear meat.

THE MALE'S MANE

Male lions have a mane for a variety of reasons. A colorful mane makes the lion more appealing to females. A thick mane helps the male to appear larger and more menacing to foes. The mane also protects the lion's throat from being bitten in a fight.

One type of physical adaptation helps animals hide in plain sight. This ability is called camouflage. Many species have adapted so their skin or fur blend in with their environments.

Panthers have black skin, making them hard to see in the dark. They are nocturnal and hunt only at night. The panthers' skin helps them sneak up on prey unnoticed.

Camouflage also explains how the grizzly bear evolved into the polar bear.

After traveling north, the grizzly's dark fur stuck out in the white surroundings. Bears with lighter hair had a better chance to survive. Over time the trait evolved into white fur.

HERE YOU GO, BUDDY.

Polar bears aren't the only animals with fur that blends in with the snowy landscape. Arctic hares and Arctic Foxes use their white fur to hide from predators, which include polar bears.

SHHH

CHAMELEON CAMOUFLAGE

Some species of chameleon have the ability to change colors as needed. A chameleon has special cells under its transparent outer skin. These cells change color to match the chameleon's environment.

IT NOT WORKING.

Mimicry is another type of physical adaptation. Mimicry is when one living thing looks or sounds like another for survival.

For example, the robber fly looks like a bumblebee. The fly even makes the same kind of buzzing sound. Predators that eat insects avoid robber flies because they fear the sting from a bumblebee.

Mimicry is also seen in the dark-footed ant-spider. This small jumping spider acts like an ant to stay safe. Most predators will not eat ants because of the tiny insects' bad taste and fighting skills.

Insects aren't the only living things that use mimicry. The milk snake is harmless, but it has the color patterns of the poisonous coral snake. The similar appearance scares away predators.

SURE HOPE IT MILK SNAKE.

Camouflage and mimicry are similar, but they have one major difference. Camouflaged creatures try to disappear into their environment. Creatures that use mimicry look and sound like living things, but they don't try to blend in.

Insects in a forest use camouflage to blend in. Although they look like living things such as leaves and tree branches, they are hiding in their environment. That means they are using camouflage, not mimicry.

CHAPTER 3

BEHAVIORAL ADAPTATIONS

Behavioral adaptations explain why animals behave in a certain way. For example, beavers gnaw on trees to sharpen their teeth. They also cut down trees to build dams.

Some animals, such as squirrels and chipmunks, can't find enough food in the winter. That's why they store nuts and acorns during the warmer months. The food they store will help them survive the winter.

Other animals have adapted behaviors to help them hunt. Some species of egrets can move easily through the water because of their thin toes.

The slow movement might attract fish that think the toes are food. If that doesn't work, the egrets will spread their wings because fish are attracted to shade.

PLAYING DEAD

When an opossum is threatened, it usually doesn't fight back. Instead, opossums "play dead." The opossum is so committed to acting dead that it can be poked, prodded, and even picked up and moved. The opossum can remain in that state for four hours. Playing dead keeps most predators at bay, since they prefer to catch their prey alive.

Birds aren't the only animals that migrate. Salmon travel from the ocean to freshwater streams to reproduce. The young then return to the ocean.

Even some insect species migrate. Monarch butterflies travel from Canada to Mexico during the winter to avoid the cold.

BIGFOOT OWE YOU ONE!

Not all animals travel long distances to escape the cold. Have you wondered why bears sleep during the winter? The answer is found in another behavioral adaptation—hibernation.

DO NOT DISTURB

Bears live in areas where it's hard to find food during the coldest months of the year. To survive, they hibernate, going into a deep sleep.

BEARS SO LAZY!

Hibernating bears don't eat for months. While asleep, their breathing slows down. Their heartbeat drops to a rate as low as eight beats a minute.

WAKE UP!!!

While hibernating, bears live on fat stored in the body. When they awaken in the spring, they are very hungry after the long winter's nap.

UH-OH.

SO ... FULL ...

FEASTING BEFORE HIBERNATION

In the summer and early fall, bears eat berries and fish to put on weight. Before they hibernate, they can gain as much as 30 pounds (13.6 kilograms) per week. After hibernation, most black bears weigh less than half their original body weight.

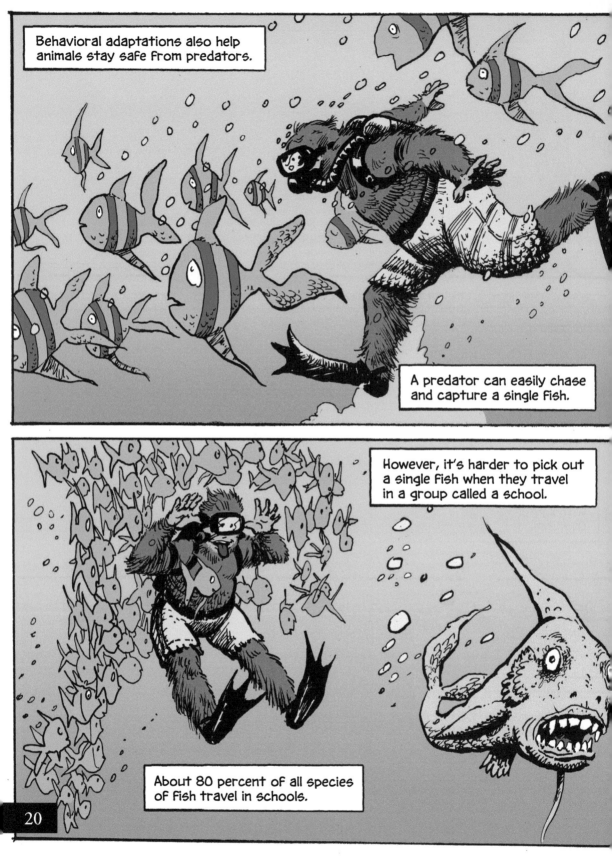

Behavioral adaptations also help animals stay safe from predators.

A predator can easily chase and capture a single fish.

However, it's harder to pick out a single fish when they travel in a group called a school.

About 80 percent of all species of fish travel in schools.

Fish aren't the only animals that use this adaptation. Deer, wolves, and elephants also live and travel in groups for safety.

AWOOOO!

Predators use a similar behavioral adaptation. For example, a lion may have trouble attacking an entire herd of zebras.

But if a lion charges and causes the herd to run, it might separate one zebra from the rest. The lion will have a better chance of bringing down a single zebra.

CHAPTER 4

ENVIRONMENTS AND ADAPTATIONS

Adaptations are a result of each species' environment. But some environments are so unfriendly that almost nothing can live there.

One example is the desert of Death Valley, California. The extreme heat during the day and frigid cold at night make it a dangerous place to live.

But plants and animals still call the desert home. The roots of the Cotton Top cactus are close to the surface. They absorb as much moisture as possible from desert rains. Sharp pointed needles protect the cactus from thirsty animals.

YOWW!!

BIGFOOT NOT GOING ANYWHERE!

Grass in the desert has long roots to help anchor it in the ground. When strong winds move the sand around the grass, it stays in place.

OOCH! AAAH! OWW!

Animals in the desert have adapted to the extreme heat in various ways. Many animals only come out at night when the temperatures have dropped. Fennec foxes have fur on their feet to protect against the sand's heat.

While the desert is extremely hot, the continent of Antarctica is very cold. Animals that live there have special features that help them survive in the low temperatures.

BIGFOOT FORGOT ELECTRIC BLANKET!

The Emperor penguin thrives in this frigid environment. This penguin stays warm with a coat made up of about 100 feathers per square inch. This thick covering provides close to 90 percent of the penguin's insulation.

The Emperor penguin has a thick layer of fat, or blubber. Both the feathers and this fat layer keep it warm in the freezing water or on land.

The penguins also huddle together to trap heat. These physical and behavioral adaptations increase their chances of survival.

Seals have blubber too. Their sleek bodies help them swim in the water.

TOC!

A seal's eyes allow it to see better underwater. When it's too dark to see, it uses its long whiskers to sense movement in the water.

Whales have both physical and behavioral adaptations. Like penguins and seals, whales use their blubber for warmth.

BIGFOOT NEED BLUBBER.

Although whales are suited for the freezing water, they migrate to warmer areas during the coldest months.

Scientists have discovered life at incredible ocean depths. Even without light, some of the most unique species on Earth have found ways to survive.

Anglerfish live at depths of 3,000 feet (914 meters), where there is little or no light. These fish have a special way of attracting prey.

A feature that looks like a light-bulb extends from its head and dangles in front of its mouth. Small creatures are drawn to the light, and the anglerfish swallows them whole.

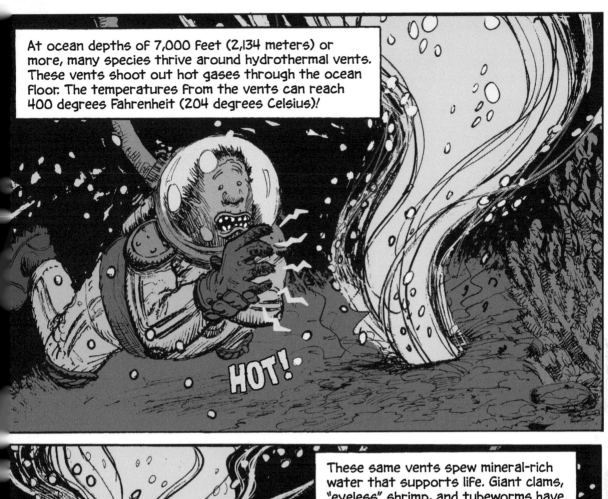

At ocean depths of 7,000 feet (2,134 meters) or more, many species thrive around hydrothermal vents. These vents shoot out hot gases through the ocean floor. The temperatures from the vents can reach 400 degrees Fahrenheit (204 degrees Celsius)!

HOT!

These same vents spew mineral-rich water that supports life. Giant clams, "eyeless" shrimp, and tubeworms have adapted to live close the vents.

NO LOOK LIKE WORMS TO ME.

Adaptations have been occurring since life began on Earth. We continue to study them as they happen today.

BIGFOOT'S INSURANCE NO COVER TESTS!

However, living creatures are sometimes unable to adapt quickly to sudden environmental changes.

If faced with drastic changes where they live, survival can become hard, or even impossible.

If living things are unable to adapt to their environments, the species will die off, or become extinct. Species that are in danger of becoming extinct are called endangered species.

BIGFOOT ENDANGERED?!?!

In order for any plant or animal to survive, it needs to adapt to its changing environment.

What adaptations will we see in the future?

29

GLOSSARY

adaptation (a-dap-TAY-shuhn)—a change a living thing goes through to better fit in with its environment

camouflage (KA-muh-flahzh)—coloring or covering that makes animals, people, and objects look like their surroundings

environment (in-VY-ruhn-muhnt)—the natural world of the land, water, and air

evolution (ev-uh-LOO-shuhn)—the change of living things over periods of time

generation (jen-uh-RAY-shuhn)—all the members of a group of people or creatures born around the same time

hibernation (hye-bur-NAY-shun)—a resting state used to survive poor conditions in the environment

insulation (in-suh-LAY-shun)—a material that stops heat, sound, or cold from entering or escaping

migration (mye-GRAY-shuhn)—the regular movement of animals as they search different places for food

mimicry (MIM-ik-ree)—a physical adaptation where a species looks like something else

nocturnal (nok-TUR-nuhl)—describes a species that is active at night and rests during the day

species (SPEE-sheez)—a group of plants or animals that share common characteristics

trait (TRATE)—a quality or characteristic that makes one person or animal different from another

transparent (transs-PAIR-uhnt)—see-through

READ MORE

Biskup, Agnieszka. *A Journey Into Adaptation with Max Axiom, Super Scientist*. Graphic Science. Mankato, Minn.: Capstone Press, 2007.

Dell, Pamela. *Surviving Death Valley: Desert Adaptation*. Extreme Life. Mankato, Minn.: Capstone Press, 2008.

Spilsbury, Richard. *Adaptation and Survival*. Living Processes. New York: Rosen Central, 2010.

INTERNET SITES

FactHound offers a safe, fun way to find Internet sites related to this book. All sites on FactHound have been researched by our staff.

Here's all you do:

Visit www.facthound.com

Type in this code: 9781429665797

Super-cool stuff! Check out projects, games and lots more at **www.capstonekids.com**

INDEX